Writers from Brazil and Portugal, Mozambique and Angola all use the same language — Portuguese, for stories from a thousand locales in a hundred styles.

Brazil — almost a continent by itself — has a tremendous set of talented writers turning over its rich tropical, urban and racial mix.

Portugal (like England) is a tiny country that has contributed far beyond its size to the world's cultural and literary wealth.

Drawing from both these traditions and their own African heritage writers from Angola and Mozambique have recently begun to chronicle their own strange story...

The Babel Guide is your way in to this wide world of reading — inside are details on *all* the novels and short stories from these countries available in English with 70 'trailers' to the best books of 35 major writers to aid your purchasing or borrowing choices.

Take a journey to the heart and soul of another world; here is the guide.

'a brilliant idea'

— BBC Radio 3

The Babel Guide
to the Fiction of
Portugal, Brazil & Africa
in English Translation

by Ray Keenoy, David Treece & Paul Hyland

with

David Brookshaw
Marina Coriolano-Lykourezos
Maria-Amelia Dalsenter
Maria-Manuela Lisboa
Tom MacCarthy
Pat Odber
Carmo Ponte
Giovanni Pontiero
Caroline Shaw

Illustrations by Jackie Wrout

BOULEVARD

Babel Guide to the Fiction of Portugal, Brazil and Africa in English Translation

©Boulevard Books 1995.
(Paul Hyland's contributions ©Paul Hyland 1995)
First published 1995 by Boulevard Books
8 Aldbourne Road
London W12 OLN, UK
Tel/Fax 0181 743 5278

Special thanks to

Michael Collins
Maria-Amelia Dalsenter
Giovanni Pontiero
Luis de Sousa Rebelo
David Treece
Siân Williams
Jackie Wrout

Published with support from the Camões Institute Lisbon,
Gulbenkian Foundation UK/Portugal 600
The publisher acknowledges financial assistance from the Arts Council of
Great Britain

ISBN 1 899460 055

Boulevard Books are distributed in the UK by Central Books.
Cover Art: Chris Hyde
Typeset & Design: Studio Europa (0181 743 5278)
Printed and bound by the Guernsey Press, Guernsey, C.I.

for Célia

CONTENTS